INSIDE

THE
AQUARIUM

INSIDE THE AQUARIUM

WRITTEN BY WENDY WAX

ILLUSTRATED BY JOE MURRAY

A CALICO BOOK

Published by Contemporary Books, Inc.

CHICAGO · NEW YORK

Library of Congress Cataloging-in-Publication Data

Wax, Wendy.
Inside the aquarium / written by Wendy Wax ;
illustrated by Joe Murray.
p.   cm.
"A Calico book."
Summary: A girl observes the work and activities in a large
metropolitan aquarium, including the feeding and breeding of animals
and the cleaning of their tanks.
ISBN 0-8092-4357-1
1. Aquariums, Public—Juvenile literature.   [1. Aquariums,
Public.]   I. Murray, Joe, ill.   II. Title.
QL78.W34   1989
639.3′4—dc19   88-37492
                                                                                    CIP
                                                                                    AC

Published by Contemporary Books, Inc.
180 North Michigan Avenue, Chicago, Illinois 60601
Manufactured in the United States of America
Library of Congress Catalog Card Number: 88-37492
International Standard Book Number: 0-8092-4357-1

Published simultaneously in Canada by Beaverbooks, Ltd.
195 Allstate Parkway, Valleywood Business Park
Markham, Ontario L3R 4T8 Canada

Special thanks to Rick Miller and Fran Hackett at the New York Aquarium in Brooklyn, New York; Bernadette Bode at the Mystic Marinelife Aquarium in Mystic, Connecticut; and Pam McCosker at the Steinhart Aquarium, California Academy of Sciences in San Francisco, California.

Early one summer Saturday morning, Polly discovered a seal washed up on the beach near her house. She ran home to tell her parents about it.

"Sometimes animals need people to help them," said Polly's father. "Be careful not to touch the seal, in case it's hurt or sick."

Polly's mother called Mr. Murray, their next-door neighbor, who worked at the aquarium. Mr. Murray said he'd send over people from the Stranding Network, a group that helps and studies stranded animals.

Soon a truck pulled up on the beach. Two workers
loaded the seal onto a stretcher and into the truck.

"What's going to happen to Oliver?" Polly asked, for
that is the name she had given the seal.

"Mr. Murray said you could go along to the aquarium
and see," her father said.

"Oh, great!" Polly said and climbed into the truck.

7

The truck drove to a back entrance of the Bay Aquarium. Mr. Murray met them at the door and led everyone into a room with a pool called a holding tank. The people from the local Stranding Network gently placed Oliver into the water. They told Mr. Murray where they found Oliver.

Mr. Murray explained to Polly that he was one of the many head keepers at the aquarium. "Head keepers feed and care for the animals. I take care of the seals and otters."

Dr. Wong, an animal doctor, came out to see Oliver.

"We'll have to give him a blood test," she said.

"Will that hurt?" Polly asked.

"Oh, no," said Dr. Wong. "We just scratch Oliver's flipper with a needle. If he's healthy, we'll have the Stranding Network return him to the ocean. If not, we'll keep him alone until he's well. We'll give him vitamins and then medicine if we have to."

"Would you like to have a look around the aquarium now?" Mr. Murray asked Polly.

"Oh, yes!" said Polly.

"Let's go see the fish first," Mr. Murray said.

9

As Mr. Murray and Polly walked into the fish gallery, Polly was amazed to see tank after tank of hundreds of different fish. There were more than she'd ever imagined! And she'd never seen such big tanks before.

The head keeper took her to the freshwater tanks. "These hold fish from lakes, ponds, and swamps," he explained.

"These are saltwater tanks," he said, pointing in another direction. "One is for sharks. Another holds marine turtles." Polly was fascinated by a creature with eight arms called an octopus.

"How do you know which fish should go in which tanks?" asked Polly.

"Well," said Mr. Murray, "some fish, like sharks, eat other fish, so they usually live only with their own kind. Also, the water temperatures are different in different tanks. The octopus needs icy-cold water. Tropical fish must live in warm water."

"I've never seen fish like these before!" Polly exclaimed.

"Look at the waves!" Polly yelled, looking into a saltwater tank.

"Those waves are made by a machine," said Mr. Murray. "Other aquariums use buckets of water that tip over when they're full. This makes the display seem like a real ocean to the fish, and to visitors."

"Does the salt water come from the ocean?" asked Polly.

"Yes, we get it through a pipeline that goes way out into the ocean and pumps the water into the aquarium."

12

Mr. Murray told Polly that all the rocks and coral reefs in the aquarium were made by humans. "Real coral reefs wouldn't live long if they were taken out of the ocean," he explained. "We make rocks and coral reefs. We even make kelp, which is a kind of seaweed, out of plastic. The fish don't know the difference. Algae and bits of food get trapped in the coral reefs even though the reefs are not real—and the fish can hide in them as if they were really in the ocean."

"Now," said Mr. Murray, "let's go see the mammals."

"We learned about mammals in school. Mammals have backbones and hair or fur. They don't lay eggs like some animals do," Polly announced proudly. "We are mammals, and so is Oliver."

The mammal section was a fun-filled area.
Killer whales, walruses, and otters were all
playing. It was better than the circus!

"Mammals are very talented," said Mr. Murray.
"The trainers don't teach them how to do these
tricks. They just give them rewards when the
animals do them right."

"I'll bet Oliver can do all of these tricks," said
Polly, smiling.

In one room, a seal was
balancing a ball on its nose.

In another room, dolphins were doing flips.

As they walked outside, Polly asked, "How do they clean the tanks, Mr. Murray? Every time I clean out my goldfish's bowl, I have to scoop him out into a cup."

"Well," he explained, "sometimes fish are scooped out with a net and placed into another tank—just like your goldfish is, only with a larger net. Usually, however, that's not necessary. The water is constantly being filtered, and that helps keep it clean.

"A staff member wipes the inside of the tanks with a sponge on the end of a stick."

"Doesn't the dirty sponge make the water dirty?" asked Polly.

"No," said Mr. Murray. "The scum that comes off the walls is filtered out of the water."

"He's cleaning the outside of the tanks with the same glass cleaner my mother uses on our windows," Polly said.

"Look, Mr. Murray!" Polly exclaimed as she watched a diver swimming in the dolphin tank. "He's cleaning the tank," said Mr. Murray. "Once a week, a diver uses a brush and sponge to clean the bottoms and the walls of the mammal tanks. Sometimes we lower the water level a little bit to make this easier."

17

At 11:00, Mr. Murray told Polly that it was feeding time. "We keep most of the food in large freezers," he said. "The food has to be thawed before it is served."

"What do the fish eat?" asked Polly. "We feed our small fish a nutritious gelatin made of chopped fish. Some fish eat fresh fish that has been cut into pieces."

"I'd hate to be the one who feeds the sharks," said Polly. "They're so scary looking."

"Sharks are fed once a day," said Mr. Murray. "Sometimes the head keeper stands on a platform above the tank, holding out squid on the end of a long metal pole."

"Twice a day, the penguins are fed fish and squid by hand. We also give the penguins and mammals vitamins."

"I take a vitamin tablet every day to get a balanced diet," said Polly.

"How about some lunch?" said Mr. Murray. "Seeing all of the animals eating has made me hungry."

They went to the outside café and ordered burgers, fries, and lemonade. While they were eating, Polly asked Mr. Murray how animals usually came to the aquarium.

"We buy most of the fish. But we often get new ones by trading with other aquariums. Sometimes these fish are ours to keep, and sometimes we only borrow them. We buy and trade so we can always have a wide variety of fish."

"Sometimes we trade baby mammals once they are old enough to be away from their mothers," Mr. Murray continued. "Often marine biologists, who are people who study animal life from the sea, bring in sick or orphaned walruses, dolphins, or seals."

"Just like Oliver," said Polly.

21

After lunch, Mr. Murray bought Polly an ice-cream cone and they headed toward the penguin house. On the way, they stopped at a door with a sign that said FISH & REPTILE BREEDING.

Passing through the door, they found a tank of baby fish. "These females keep their eggs and newly hatched young in their mouths until the babies are ready to be on their own," said Mr. Murray.

A tank of green turtles was also in the breeding room. "Female green turtles lay about a hundred eggs at a time. Only a few of them become babies though," he said. "We're one of the few aquariums that raises turtles."

"I thought lobsters were supposed to be red," said Polly, looking into a tank of blue lobsters.

"Not always," said Mr. Murray. "A group of fishermen brought us blue lobsters from the ocean. We put them into our red-lobster tank, and to everybody's surprise, these beautiful blue baby lobsters were born."

"Oliver's a baby seal, isn't he?" asked Polly.

"Oliver is a pup, which is what we call a baby seal. He's only a few weeks old," said Mr. Murray. "Come on. Maybe we can see some baby penguins. Baby penguins are called chicks."

At the penguin house, adult penguins and chicks were everywhere. "Penguins have chicks every year," Mr. Murray explained. "A penguin colony is a very tight family unit, so aquariums don't trade penguins back and forth much."

He told Polly that penguins are known as marine birds. "They use their wings as flippers to swim. They can't fly," he said.

"They like to toboggan, too," Polly laughed, as she saw a penguin sliding on its belly down icy hills.

"These are Adélie penguins, which come from Antarctica."

"My teacher showed us pictures of Antarctica. This looks like a mini-Antarctica!" Polly said.

"We want the penguins to feel at home, so we make ice structures—rocks, boulders, and cracks—for them to live in. Some of the structures are real, and some are artificial."

Polly shivered. "It's cold in here."

"The head keeper makes sure the temperature is always cold enough to keep ice from melting," said Mr. Murray. "Come on. We'd better leave before you catch cold."

Mr. Murray said they should start heading back. On their way, they passed the back-up area. "This is where sick animals are taken," said Mr. Murray.

They walked in and saw Dr. Lee, another animal doctor, sitting next to a stretcher with a seal lying on it. The seal's flippers were covered with small bumps.

"He looks like he has the chicken pox," said Polly.

"Seal pox," said the animal doctor. "I found it while I was giving the mammals their checkups, which I do every three or four months. Now that he's taking medicine, he'll be healthy in no time." Dr. Lee explained to Polly what was done during a checkup.

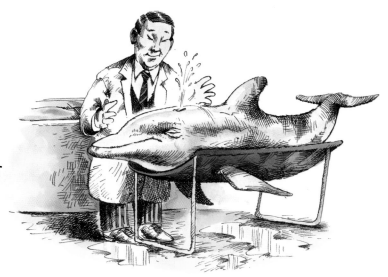

"The mammals are taken out of the water and placed on these stretchers. We test their blood, their breathing, and their skin. If they're sick, they are given medicine."

"The dolphin in that holding tank is sick and must be given medicine for the next week," said Dr. Lee.

"It's harder to tell if turtles and fish are sick. The head keeper checks for signs that they are not well when he or she looks in the tanks. If there's a problem, the food and water must also be checked."

They left the back-up area, and Mr. Murray introduced Polly to some of the aquarium workers. There were college and high school students who worked at the information booth for the summer.

She met a group of tour guides. Some spoke foreign languages so that people from other countries could understand the tour, too.

A man told Polly that he was a lab technician, which meant that he tested the water quality and treated the tanks if there was a problem.

A marine biologist explained that she did research in the aquarium.

"I think I'd like to work here when I get older," said Polly.

Inside the gift shop, Polly looked at coral jewelry, stuffed penguins, and dolphin calendars. When they left the gift shop, Mr. Murray handed her a box. Inside was a coral necklace with a seal charm dangling from it.

"What a wonderful present!" she said. "It looks just like Oliver! Thank you."

When they returned to the building where they'd left Oliver, they found him swimming playfully.

"Oliver!" called Polly. He came up out of the water and barked happily.

Dr. Wong said Oliver was in perfect health. "This means he'll be returned to his true home—the ocean. I've called the people at the Stranding Network to come and pick him up."

Polly was sad, but she said, "Oliver, even though I'll miss you, I know you'll be happy once you get back in the ocean." He barked again as Polly headed outside where her parents were waiting for her, for it was time to go.

EMPLOYEE'S EXIT

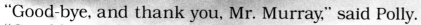

"Good-bye, and thank you, Mr. Murray," said Polly.
"Good-bye, Polly," he said. "Why don't you come back next Saturday?"
"I think I will!"
On the way home Polly told her parents about her exciting day at the aquarium.